# Self-Esteem

Unleash Your Inner Strength A Straightforward Guide To Regaining Your Confidence And Raising Your Self-Esteem

(Quick And Easy Ways To Improve Your Self-Esteem)

**Lorenzo Rutherford**

# TABLE OF CONTENT

Introduction ............................................................. 1

Chapter 1: Exclusive Access To Friendships. ............. 4

Chapter 2: Fear And Reason. ........................................... 13

Chapter 3: How To Increase Our Self-Worth ............ 24

Chapter 4: Indisputable Indicators Of Inferiority Complex ..................................................................... 34

Chapter 5: Boosting One's Own Confidence ............. 39

Chapter 6: How Negative Thoughts Influence One's Self-Esteem ..................................................................... 54

Chapter 7: How To Conquer Low Self-Esteem And Cultivate High Self-Esteem ............................................. 61

Chapter 8: What Your Adolescent Daughter Is Hiding From You .................................................................. 70

Chapter 9: Developing The Right Attitude ................ 79

Chapter 9: Do Not Contrast Yourself With Others And The World Around You. .......................................... 110

Chapter 10: Comprehensive Therapeutic Assistance For Low Self-Esteem ....................................................... 120

Chapter 11: Avoiding The Negative Behaviors That Will Ruin Your Child's Life ............................................. 130

## Introduction

There is a very solid explanation for why self-esteem issues are becoming increasingly prevalent. It's not surprising that some people believe they don't live up to society's expectations, given the increase in divorce rates and the pressure placed on individuals to succeed. It is difficult to be perfect, yet we see flawless individuals on magazine covers and on television. We also see advertisements for all the products that can assist us in conforming to these standards, but the majority of them are bogus.

So, if you have a problem with the way you view yourself, how can you overcome this negative perspective?

Regarding this, the investigation was conducted. We are confident that the strategies outlined in these pages will assist you in overcoming feelings of self-loathing. They will also help you develop self-assurance so that you can confront the world with optimism and positivity.

The strategies employed in this book have been demonstrated to be effective, and it will be worthwhile to attempt each one in turn because each one boosts your confidence levels, and one may not be sufficient on its own. Consequently, peruse the book. Try the exercises we've suggested, and you'll see yourself in a new perspective. You will recognize your own worth and no longer require others to validate who you are. This is significant because individuals with self-esteem issues perpetually seek external validation. You must immediately cease doing that because even if others validate you, it does little for your self-esteem. In the end, this is the only opinion that matters, as it is the one you must live with.

We will teach you how to succeed and feel good about yourself by intentionally shunning external validation. The only person whose sanction is required for the exercises in this experiment is you. Develop a positive outlook on your interactions with others. Learn to appreciate yourself. That is the purpose of existence, and once you realize it, you will never again feel inadequate.

## Chapter 1: Exclusive Access To Friendships.

"When fifty-one percent of the choosers believe in cooperation as opposed to competition, the Ideal Commonwealth will cease to be a proposition and become a reality," said a distinguished individual with whom I am acquainted.

That man should work together for the benefit of all is truly beautiful, and I believe the day will come when these effects are realized, but the simple act of 51% of the electorate voting for illiberalism will not bring it about.

Voting is merely the expression of an opinion, and after the votes have been counted there is still work to be completed. The majority of the time, a male may behave in an idiotic manner.

The bitter, combative, avaricious, and covetous communist is constructing an opposition that will keep him and others like him in check. And this opposition is justified, as a genuinely corrupt society is compelled to protect itself from dissolution and deterioration. To take over monopolies and operate them for the benefit of society is not sufficient, nor is it desirable, so long as the concept of the competition is complete.

As long as tone is paramount in men's minds, they will sweat and despise other men, and under illiberalism there would be exactly the same struggle for position and power that we observe in contemporary politics.

Reconstructing society is impossible until its members are reconstructed.

Mankind must be reborn. When fifty-one percent of the choosers rule their spirit and remove fifty-one percent of their current covetousness, bitterness, hatred, fear, and foolish pride from their hearts, and only then, illiberalism will arrive.

The topic is far too vast to be addressed in a single paragraph, so I will limit myself to a single example: the danger to society posed by exclusive FRIENDSHIPS between men and men and women and women and women. No two people with the same coitus can encircle each other, nor can they support or benefit one another. Typically, they distort the internal and spiritual state of affairs. We should have many or no commonalities. When two males "tell each other everything," they are approaching caducity. There must be some clearly delineated reserve. We're told that in the instance of a solid sword, the motes cannot touch. They never surrender their uniqueness. We are all specks of Divinity, and we should not abandon our individuality. Be yourself; no man should be required of you. Your friend will think more highly of you if you maintain some distance. Fellowship, like credit, is most prestigious when not utilized.

I can comprehend how a robust man can have a deep and abiding affection for a thousand other men and call them all by name, but I cannot fathom how he can regard one of these men as more advanced than the others while maintaining his internal equilibrium.

If a man is close enough, he will hold you as if you were drowning, and you will both go down. In an intimate and exclusive fellowship, males partake in the sins of others.

In shops and factories, it is common for males to be accompanied by others. These men openly discuss their difficulties with one another; they do not withhold any information; they express mutual sympathy and condole.

They collaborate and support one another. Their association is exclusive, and others recognize this. Covetousness seeps in, doubt reawakens, and loathing lurks around the corner, and these men develop a collective distaste for particular effects and individuals. By feting their difficulties, men bring them to life, thereby provoking each other and diluting reason. Effects become obscured, and a sense of worth is lost. By permitting someone to be an adversary, you transform him into one.

Soon, others will join us, and we will have a throng. A throng is an abandoned fellowship.

A multitude develops into a body, and a body into a feud, and before long, we have a mob, which is an eyeless, stupid, insane, crazy, rampaging, and roaring mass that has lost its direction. There are no individuals in a mob because everyone is of one mentality, and independent study has ceased.

A feud is based on nothing; it is a mistake, a blunder, and a foolish notion hammered into honey by a foolish friend! And a throng may form.

Every man who has participated in collaborative life has observed that the crowd is the disintegrating bacillus, and that the crowd always arises from the exclusive fellowship of two persons of the same coitus, who tell each other all unkind effects that are said about the other; therefore, be cautious. Protect the elite fellowship! Respect all men and look for the virtue in each one. It is foolish to associate only with the sociable, the humorous, the wise, and the brilliant; instead, associate with the simple, the ignorant, and the uneducated and exercise your own wit and intelligence. You grow by giving; you hold your friend as much by keeping your distance from him as by following him.

Respect him, but be natural and allow space to intervene. Be an exemplary repair.

Give your friend an opportunity to be himself by being yourself. Therefore, benefit him, and benefit yourself by serving him.

The greatest coziness exists between those who can live without one another.

Certainly, there have been instances of exclusive friendship that have been presented to us as grand examples of affection, but these instances are so rare and exceptional that they serve to highlight the fact that it is extremely unwise for men of average power and intelligence to consider their fellow men as friends. Many men who are large enough to have a place in history might be able to play the role of David to another's Jonathan while retaining the goodwill of all, but the greatest among us would breed animosity and strife.

And this beautiful dream of illiberalism, in which everyone works for the benefit of all, will never be realized until fifty-one percent of adults abandon all exclusive comfort. Until then, you will encounter sets, appellations that are sets grown into large coalitions, feuds, and occasional riots.

Do not lean on anyone, and spare no bone for yourself. The perfect society will consist of perfect individuals. Be a gentleman and a friend to all.

When the Master admonished his disciples to love their enemies, he was mindful of the fact that an exclusive love is erroneous. Love perishes when monopolized. It increases by sharing. Your adversary misunderstands you, so why don't you rise above the mist, recognize his error, and admire him for the qualities you find in him?

## Chapter 2: Fear And Reason.

"In civilized life, it is now possible for large numbers of people to go from the cradle to the grave without experiencing a single moment of genuine dread. "Many of us require an assault of internal complaint to teach us the meaning of the term.The author William James.

We've all heard the purportedly divergent assertions that sweat is normal and abnormal, and that normal fear should be regarded as an ally while aberrant fear should be eradicated.

In actuality, it is impossible to identify a so-called "normal" dread that has not been exhibited by some individuals who have had every reason to feel it.

Nonetheless, if you run through mortal history in your mind or look around you in the present life, you will discover then and their people. They retain every emotion and permission except terror. The concept of tone- preservation is as explosively present among the most modestly apprehensive or alarmed individuals, but they are unaware. This courageous awareness of anxiety suggests that conditions may have multiple causes. It may result from indigenous make-up, extended, uninterrupted training, heroinism, religious elation, an unshakeable, impeccably calm sense of spiritual identity, or the operation of genuinely elevated reason. Regardless of the explanation, it is undeniable that the causes that provoke fear in the majority of us merely appeal, with similar individuals, if at all, to the instinct of tone-preservation and to reason, the study-element of the soul that promotes peace and wholeness.

Eliminate all anxiety.

On the basis of similar considerations, I've come to believe that all true fear-feeling should and can be eradicated from our lives, and that what we refer to as "normal fear" should be replaced in our language by "instinct" or "reason," with the element of fear eliminated.

"Everyone can affirm that the psychological state known as fear is composed of internal representations of certain painful outcomes" (James). The internal representations of similarity may be extremely subtle, but the concept of harm to tone is present. However, it is also possible to have a profound belief that the true tone cannot be damaged; if the mind can be brought to vividly and credibly contemplate all quieting considerations; if the tone can be held purposefully in the knowledge that the White Life surrounds the true tone.

These are also the ways in which any cause for dread can be subdivided.

As both a warning and a source of dread. Let us say, however, that the warning should be interpreted as being given to reason, that fear need not manifest at each, and that fear is utterly pointless suffering. With these distinctions in mind, we can now proceed to the primary investigation of fear.

primary research into dread.

Fear is an impulse, a routine, and a complaint.

Fear, as it exists in humans, is a rational fabrication, a figment of the imagination, and a condition of lunacy.

Similarly, dread is composed of the jitters, the mind, and the moral knowledge.

The division depends on one's perspective. Reason should replace what is commonly referred to as normal fear, using the term to encompass instinct as well as study. From the proper perspective, all terror is wrong so long as it is entertained.

Regardless of its manifestations or apparent location, fear is a psychic state that manifests itself in a variety of ways, such as in the jitters, internal moods, a single impulse, a habitual routine, or a wholly unstable condition. The response is always positive, signifying, in each instance, "Be careful! Danger!" This is the case if you consider three comprehensive types of fear: dread of tone, fear for tone, and fear for others. apprehension of tone is an indirect apprehension of tone danger. As a result of anticipated misfortune on the part of others, a person's irrational fear of them entails presupposed or previsualized pain. In our research, I frequently question whether when we sweat for others, we are causing them the most torment or pain.

Fear is also commonly regarded as the soul's danger signal. The true signal, however, is thoughtful spontaneity.

Instinct and reason, when functioning as a warning, can perform their duties abnormally or assume abnormal proportions. In addition, we experience anxiety. The standard warning is supported by factual danger and a mind in a state of equilibrium and self-control. Normal intellect is always capable of analogous forewarning. There are only two methods to eradicate so-called normal fear acting under the guise of reason: the negotiation of fear for reason and the assurance of a white life.

Now let it be understood that by normal fear is meant that normal reason genuine fear is denied any place or function. Additionally, we can say that the analogous action of reason is a donor to humanity. It is, with suffering and fatigue, the altruism of our nature of effects.

One person said, "Exhausted? No synonyms allowed in my home!" This station cannot be sound and wholesome. At a certain stage of difficulty, weariness is a signal to cease activity. When one becomes so engrossed in work that he loses awareness of the sensation of fatigue, he has issued a "hurry call" to mortality. I do not deny that the soul can cultivate a sublime sense of buoyancy and power; in fact, I encourage you to pursue this beautiful condition. However, I maintain that when a belief or a daydream prevents you from hearing the warning of jitters and muscles, Nature will inevitably bring about calamity. Let us stand for the greater liberty that is jubilantly free to utilize everything Nature has to offer for genuine well-being. There is a partial liberty that attempts to realize itself by denying colorful realities as real, and there is an advanced liberty that actually realizes itself by admitting similar realities as real and by using or disusing them as the occasion demands in the interest of the tone at its most stylistic. I consider it true prudence to take advantage of everything that ostensibly promises good for the tone, without regard to any particular proposition, and to freely utilize all effects, whether material, immaterial, rational, or spiritual. I accept your wisdom or your system, but I implore you to disregard your devotion to the gospel or to thickness. Therefore, I assert that the sick feeling is a rational command to replenish depleted nerves and muscles in individuals with normal health.

It is neither free nor healthy to proclaim, "There's no pain!" Pain exists, regardless of what you assert, and your protestation that it does not is evidence that it does, for why (and how) would you assert the virtuality of something that is actually absent? But if you say, "I have pain, but I'm working hard to ignore it and cultivate study-health so that the source of my pain can be eliminated," that is stable and beautiful. This is the enviable position of the biblical figure who cried out, "Lord, I believe; help my unbelief!" To bear suffocating agony with a haze of mental haze is to become a challenger against the good government of Nature. By means of suffering, Nature informs the existing being that he is nearly inoperable. This alert is typical. The sensation becomes abnormal in the mind when the imagination twangs the jitters with repeated vexation and the will, confused by the discord and psychic chaos, cowers and jitters in dread.

I do not claim that there is nothing comparable to anxiety. Fear does exist. However, it only exists in your existence with your permission and not as a warning against "wrong."

Fear is induced by exaggerating actual danger or by conjuring fictitious threats through excessive and misguided psychical responses. This may also be interpreted as a sign of danger, but it is a falsely-intentioned substantiation because it isn't required, is hostile to the individual because it threatens tone-control, and diverts life's forces from creating values to pointless and destructive work.

## Chapter 3: How To Increase Our Self-Worth

To increase self-esteem, it requires effort, perseverance, and a desire to investigate and challenge negative self-talk and actively reinforce positive self-thoughts. Having grace for yourself is essential. You must let go of what irritates you and concentrate on what you can (and wish to) change.

If you have adequate self-respect and self-appreciation, you will also recognize that you deserve to take care of yourself, which could motivate you to work on boosting your self-esteem. It is difficult to take care of yourself if you do not value yourself.

Self-forgiveness may also contribute to an elevated sense of self-worth.

It boils down to accepting and loving yourself exactly as you are.

To establish a self-esteem baseline, conduct a self-esteem survey.
It may be as simple as identifying your top ten strengths and ten weaknesses. This will help you begin to form an accurate and realistic image of yourself.

Establish reasonable objectives.
Setting modest, manageable, and attainable objectives is essential. Setting unrealistic expectations or expecting another person to change their behavior, for example, is almost certain to make you feel deficient despite the fact that you have done nothing wrong.

Give up your pursuit of perfection.
Recognize both your strengths and your weaknesses. No one is perfect, and endeavoring to be so will only lead to disappointment. The key to maintaining

a positive outlook while learning from your errors is to recognize both your accomplishments and your shortcomings.

Consider who you are.
It is essential to know yourself and be at ease with who you are. It may require some trial and error, and you will perpetually learn new things about yourself, but you should embark on this journey with vigor and purpose.

5. Be open to altering your self-perception.
Adapting to our ever-changing selves as we age and develop is necessary if we are to create and achieve meaningful objectives.

6. Cease comparing yourself to others.

It is very easy to fall into the comparison trap, particularly in the era of social media and the ability to present a polished, flawless image.

Here are some additional helpful tips for boosting your self-esteem:
- Inform your inner critic to cease.

Adopt more effective motivational techniques.
- Take a two-minute break to appreciate yourself.
- Write down three positive characteristics about yourself that you can appreciate in the evening.
- Take the appropriate action.
- Find a replacement for perfectionism.
- Approach mistakes and disappointments with greater optimism.
- Exhibit courtesy toward others.
- Be adventurous.

Avoid falling victim to the comparison fallacy.

- Spend more time with those who are uplifting (and less time with those who are detrimental).

# Chapter 3

## Factors that affect adolescents' self-esteem

An adolescent's low self-esteem can be a significant burden. Teens with low self-esteem are susceptible to being harassed, bullying others, abusing drugs and alcohol, and considering suicide. Building a teenager's self-esteem is a gradual and difficult process, but if you can identify the factors influencing her self-perception, you'll know where to begin.

### Body Image

The onset of puberty can be detrimental to a teen's self-esteem. When her body begins to change, she may begin to feel self-conscious about these alterations and how she's maturing in comparison to her peers. A man may experience embarrassment if he becomes smaller than his peers, while a woman may experience humiliation if her breasts swell and she attracts unwanted attention from elderly men. As she begins to develop crushes on other people, a teen will become more concerned with her appearance than she was as a youngster. If she is unable to purchase the most popular clothing or is larger or smaller than prominent artists and actresses, she may feel inferior to her peers and to celebrities.

The onset of puberty can be detrimental to a teen's self-esteem.
As she begins to develop crushes on other people, a teen will become more concerned with her appearance than she was as a youngster.

The Importance of Belonging in Teenage Social Experiences.

Both a teen's family and academic environment will impact his self-esteem. If he is reared in a loving and nurturing home and has a close-knit group of supportive school friends, his self-esteem may be higher than that of a child whose parents are critical and who has few friends. Being harassed or shunned by peers or reprimanded by teachers can also lower a teen's self-esteem. If a person has a physical or mental disability or is of a different race or religion than the majority of his classmates, he may experience embarrassment and shame, which may lead to low self-esteem.

Both a teen's family and academic environment will impact his self-esteem.

If a person has a physical or mental disability or is of a different race or religion than the majority of his classmates, he may experience embarrassment and shame, which may lead to low self-esteem.

Performance

Some students will be unfazed by failing algebra, while others will be devastated by receiving a B on an exam. Beyond academic achievement, a child's extracurricular activities will affect his self-image, sometimes for the better and sometimes for the worse. A child may feel humiliated if he is not selected for a team, whereas being selected and joining a team can make him feel essential and respected. Encourage him to pursue his passions, as doing so can have a significant impact on his self-esteem. Teens' self-esteem can be boosted through community service initiatives.

One's Voice

No matter how attractive, educated, or successful a person is, a teenager may be unable to recognize all of his/her assets and instead focus on his/her flaws. One's perceptions of his place in the universe and the things he/she tells him/herself will influence how they value themselves. In contrast, an adolescent who lies in the middle of the pack in terms of appearance and social status may have a positive self-image due to a positive internal monologue. You cannot persuade a child with low self-esteem that he or she is valuable and enjoyable to be around by simply telling him or her once. Over time, praising his/her efforts and providing constructive feedback in lieu of criticism can help him/her alter some of his/her negative self-perceptions.

## Chapter 4: Indisputable Indicators Of Inferiority Complex

The subconscious desire to be accepted and acknowledged conflicts with the individual's great dread of embarrassment, which prevents them from being themselves. The term for this is inferiority complex. He is anxious about derision and humiliation. He fears making errors and being harmed by what others will say about him because of his faults. Listed below are signs that you may have an inferiority complex:

You assign responsibility. You begin to act irrationally when you blame others for your errors and misfortune. It is inappropriate to hold others accountable for one's own mistakes. You are displaying signs of an inferiority complex when your mind constantly tells you that they are deliberately trying to make you fail.

Your behavior is hypocritical. You fail to recognize the positive qualities of others. You can only recognize their flaws. Even though you feel poorly about yourself, you want others to feel the same way. You search for flaws in their work in order to convince yourself that they are less competent than you.

You believe they are attempting to injure you. You believe that they are making every effort to destroy you. When someone says or does something you dislike, you have a tendency to exaggerate the situation and believe they are threatening your life. You refuse to acknowledge that you are responsible for the direction of your existence.

You take feedback personally. You recognize that you are responsible for what occurred, but you do not wish to hear the truth from others. You perceive their perspectives as personal attacks. Consider that they are constantly attempting to make light of you. You disregard constructive criticism and believe that others criticize you solely to make you feel terrible.

You lack the courtesy required to accept compliments. You are unsure of how to respond when someone compliments you on a commendable act. You believe they are simply being polite. In other situations, you need a great deal of flattery to persist. In an effort to persuade yourself that you are a good person, you are desperately pursuing affirmation and compliments.

You steer clear of competition. You avoid fame-threatening situations and public displays of your skills as much as possible, not because you lack the ability to succeed, but because you believe you will. Worse still, you don't even show up in order to avoid being a participant.

You attempt to avoid being seen in public frequently. You avoid public places because you believe you are inferior to other individuals. You refrain from expressing your opinions and remain reticent on issues that are significant to you. You lead a secluded existence and avoid attracting others' notice. You do not believe your skills will distinguish you or that the world will care about you.

You are excessively anxious. You doubt your ability to complete a mission. You begin to fear that competition will result in negative outcomes. You are concerned that people will ridicule your efforts. You begin to feel agitated and despondent. If you allow extreme anxiety to consume you, you risk developing melancholy and compromising your mental health.

You surround yourself with walls based on your accomplishment. You exert considerable effort in pursuit of success and wealth so that others do not perceive you as insecure and feeble. You endeavor to be the best in your field of expertise to conceal your flaws and weaknesses. 10. You place yourself above others. People with inferiority complexes utilize this as a protective mechanism. You begin to criticize other people. In whatever they do, faults are always apparent.

## Chapter 5: Boosting One's Own Confidence

How can we assist our children in developing a wholesome self-image?

In general, children must perceive that their growth and development are consistent with their age and developmental stage. Due to education, some individuals may believe that this is not true.

What then can we do to aid at home?

i. The assertions we make.

Some of the phrases we use, such as "you almost made me jump out of my skin" and "I'm so hungry I could eat a horse," can be quite frightening to very young children. There are numerous ways in which we may unwittingly teach our children negative things about themselves, especially when we are angry and screaming at them. When you consider how statements such as "You should be ashamed of yourself" or "why can't you just behave?" might sound to a child, they become depressing.

ii. Respect each child's unique temperament

Keep in mind that everyone, especially youthful people, sees the world differently.

A child of age eight might find a way to catch tadpoles in a drawer of saucepans, but a child of age three will unquestionably find a way to play the drums. Although you see them as being for dinner preparation, they can be used for either purpose. Although the drum set is obnoxious and noisy, it is also entertaining and inventive. The eight-year-old's tadpole catcher is unsanitary and possibly too weighty, but it demonstrates an interest in learning and the natural world. Despite their striking contrasts, both desires are equally intense.

It is essential to ensure that everyone has the opportunity to use the saucepans (so to speak) in order to create a balanced environment for everyone. As you play the percussion set while seated on the floor, brace yourself for the volume. Applaud the inventive play and join in. Make tadpole hunting an adventure by actively seeking them out. Let your child know how pleased you are that he is so interested in learning about the metamorphosis of tadpoles into frogs, and how entertaining it will be to watch them develop as a result of his enthusiasm. Obviously, you should then thoroughly cleanse your saucepans!

Even if you don't understand or share a specific interest, your child cares about it and wants you to care as well. You may nurture and direct them so long as they share their passions and thoughts with you.

THE LITTLE THINGS MATTER AND MAKE A DIFFERENCE.

Every parent can take daily steps to help their school-aged child cope with the inevitable challenges they will face.

Applaud the process rather than the result. It may be distressing for your child to put forth a great deal of effort and still fall short. You can exhibit your pride in them for their hard work by drawing attention to it. As long as they gave it their all, you can be contented with the outcome.

Permit them to express their discontent. It is acceptable to feel disappointed if you lose the bag race when you are five. They will continue to weep even if you tell them not to be so stupid because you're embarrassed by their tears on sports day.

Permit them to express their emotions, then acknowledge them and conclude with a motivating statement: "I understand you're upset about the contest, and that's okay. But do you recall last year, when you were unable to even jump? You have now qualified for third place! It's amazing to see how far you've come in such a brief amount of time. Recognizing and identifying an emotion makes it much easier to manage.

Accept that they will base their decisions on the opinions of their peers, but reassure them of their unique value. They possibly were

They were picked last for the football team, but that's alright because they're great runners. If you can make them feel proud of their unique qualities, they will always have something to offset the negative.

Physical engagement. A significant expression of affection for children is an embrace, holding their hand, or even brushing their hair. The consideration of other responsible adults. Individual attention and interaction with other adults, such as assisting a neighbor in the garden, going on a bike ride with an uncle, or learning to fish with Grandpa, boost children's self-esteem significantly.

The idle period. It is tempting to join every available group in the aspirations of becoming well-rounded young adults. To fully decompress and relax, children must spend time at home in a familiar environment.

Exclusive time spent with you. Although it may appear simple, administering it is more difficult than it may appear. Children enjoy bedtime because they have your undivided attention. You are not checking your phone, viewing supper, or ironing anything in their bedroom while you read them a bedtime story.

Make them believe that something or someone improved AS A RESULT OF THEIR ACTIONS. I'm so glad you came over after work to give Daddy that enormous embrace; it cheered him up. Demonstrate that they have the same capacity to influence your disposition and day as you do.

Your time is the most important resource your child requires from you to develop a healthy sense of self. We may be materially wealthy, but we lack leisure. Even more so in today's technology-driven society. Be available and free of obligations to provide daily time for peaceful study. Yes, it may be difficult if you are working and have a large number of tasks to complete, but it only takes 10 minutes and will have a significant impact on your child.

What occurs when you are not present?

Sending a child to school when you are aware of their instability can be devastating. The good news is that you can assist them in constructing a robust "force field" that will protect them from the words and actions of others.

You can assist them in developing a highly potent idea that will inspire confidence in any circumstance. This may be a fond memory or something they anxiously anticipate, such as a vacation or a new toy. To help them remember this concept, request that they enumerate all the positive emotions associated with it. If they are too immature to write about it, they may instead draw a picture. It will provide them with something to focus on and genuine comfort.

Teach children the importance and benefits of maintaining personal boundaries. Provide them with well-rehearsed phrases to use in your absence, such as "Please stop, I don't like that" and "I don't want you to do that, it makes me feel horrible." Demonstrate to children how words can transform situations, even when used negatively against them.

Give them a physical reminder, such as a humorous family photograph they can carry in their pocket. When anxious, they can use it as an anchor to recall pleasant thoughts and memories by placing their hand on it.

SHOW OFF THEIR ABILITY.

Lastly, it is essential to let your child know how capable they are, as this will significantly boost their sense of self-worth and enable you to lavish them with sincere praise as they feel proud of themselves. Consider modesty and emulate their behavior.

You Can Achieve This Using the Following Methods:

Organizing items, such as sorting clean laundry according to whose it is. They can assist you in accomplishing this simple endeavor. Other examples include creating a meal and organizing a cluttered bookcase.

Giving someone total control over something is known as influence. Permitting them to choose their clothing or the color of their new bedroom, for example.

Cooking is wonderful because it requires a variety of skills. They use time management, measurement arithmetic, reading, and creativity to produce a delectable product that they can share with others.

Family games can teach them the valuable lesson that although they may not always be successful, the effort they put forth and the happiness it brings to others is just as meaningful and satisfying.

Permitting them to make mistakes; not preventing them from doing so beforehand. They must because doing so will enable them to mature and learn from their errors. Your brain grows through experience, so allowing yourself to make mistakes can help you relax and be more willing to try new activities.

A sense of pride for one's lineage.

Since a child's self-esteem develops initially within the family, the beliefs and perceptions of the family as a whole have a substantial effect on that growth. The family's self-esteem can be enhanced by implementing some of the above recommendations. Keep in mind that family pride is essential to self-esteem and can be fostered and maintained in a variety of ways, such as by participating in community events, researching one's ancestry, and caring for extended family members.

Families fare better when members focus on one another's positive qualities, refrain from severe criticism, and publicly defend one another. Members of the family embrace one another's distinct differences, have faith in one another, and display affection. They set aside time to spend with one another, whether for festivities, special occasions, or simple enjoyment.

# Chapter 6: How Negative Thoughts Influence One's Self-Esteem

You may be sending yourself negative internal messages. Many individuals do. These are the lessons you learned when you were young. You gained knowledge from a variety of sources, including other children, your educators, relatives, parental figures, the media, and bias and disgrace in our general population. You may have repeated these negative messages to yourself repeatedly after learning them, especially when you were not feeling well or when you were struggling. They may have earned your trust. You may have even exacerbated the situation by creating your own negative messages or thoughts. These negative thoughts or messages make you regret your actions and lower your self-esteem.

People frequently repeat negative messages to themselves, such as "I'm a jerk," "I'm a loser," "I never do anything right," "No one could ever like me," and "I'm a klutz." The majority of people embrace these messages regardless of how false or implausible they are. When you discover an incorrect answer, you may think, "I'm so stupid." They may contain words such as ought to, should, or should. The messages will frequently depict the most horrifyingly horrible things, including you, and they are difficult to turn off or forget.

You may have these thoughts or send yourself these negative messages so often that you are unaware of them. Concentrate on them. Carry a small notepad with you as you go about your daily routine for a few days and jot down any regrettable thoughts you have about yourself whenever they occur to you. Certain individuals assert that they exhibit more regrettable reasoning when they are exhausted, weakened, or under a great deal of stress. As you become more aware of your negative thoughts, you may observe more of them.

It aids in determining the validity of your examples of negative ideas by assisting with their investigation. You could argue that a close friend or instructor should assist you with this. When you are feeling good and have a positive self-perspective, ask yourself the following questions regarding each negative thought you have recorded.

Is this message actually unambiguous?

Could a person communicate this to another? If not, why am I communicating this to myself?

What do I avoid when considering this concept? Why should I continue to consider it if it causes me to feel negatively about myself?

You could also ask another person, someone who favors you and whom you trust, if you should believe this notion about yourself. Frequently, merely examining a concept or circumstance from a different perspective can have a significant impact.

The next step in this cycle is to develop positive affirmations that you can share with yourself to replace these negative thoughts whenever you become aware of having them. You cannot simultaneously contemplate two factors. When you are forming a positive opinion of yourself, you must not entertain a negative opinion. Utilize positive terms such as euphoric, tranquil, cherishing, energizing, and warm when promoting these considerations.

Avoid using negative language, such as stressed, terrified, irritated, drained, fatigued, not, never, can't. Try to avoid phrases such as "I won't stress anymore." Instead, say "I focus on the good" or whatever feels natural to you. Substitute "it would be fantastic if" for "should." Always use the current state, e.g., "I am healthy, I am happy, I have a steady job," as though the condition currently exists. Use I or my name, or yours.

This can be accomplished by collapsing a sheet of paper into two sections using a portion of the long method. In one section, write a negative idea, and in the other, a positive idea that contradicts the negative idea, as shown on the following page.

You can make progress toward replacing negative thoughts with positive ones by:


Substituting the negative thought with a positive one whenever you realize you are thinking of the negative thought.


Repeating your positive thought repeatedly to yourself, without reluctance, whenever you have the chance and, surprisingly, sharing it with someone else if possible.


Repeatedly maintaining communication with them.

creating signs with the positive thought, placing them where you will see them frequently, such as on your refrigerator or bathroom mirror, and repeating the thought to yourself several times when you see the sign.

It helps to reinforce the positive thought if you repeat it to yourself repeatedly when you are deeply relaxed, such as when you are doing deep breathing or a relaxing activity, or when you are simply dozing off or waking up. Changing negative self-thoughts into positive ones requires patience and diligence. If you use the following techniques consistently for four to four and a half months, you will notice you have fewer negative thoughts about yourself. You can repeat these exercises if the problems arise again in the future. Try not to give up. You have the freedom to engage in profound self-reflection.

In conclusion, these concepts are just the beginning of the journey. As you work on boosting your self-esteem, you will notice that you feel better more frequently, that you are participating in your life more than before, and that you are completing a greater number of the tasks that you have needed to do for practically forever.

## Chapter 7: How To Conquer Low Self-Esteem And Cultivate High Self-Esteem

Developing high self-esteem is not an easy task, but it is certainly possible and within your control, and it can have a profound impact on your life. As stated previously, it is essential to recognize that a significant portion of self-esteem is based on your thought patterns, what you focus on, and your optimism, as opposed to merely your actual circumstances or life events. Work, confidence, and a willingness to examine and contradict negative self-contemplations — as well as effectively reinforce your positive self-image — are required for effective self-image management. It is essential to provide yourself with ease, to let go of specific things that aggravate you, and to work on those areas that you can (and must) alter. Assuming you value yourself and have a sufficient amount of self-worth, you also recognize that you have the right to take care of yourself, which can contribute to your efforts to improve your self-esteem. It is difficult to manage yourself when you ponder ineffectively about yourself.

Focuses on demonstrating that forgiving yourself for things you regret can also aid in further developing self-esteem.26 Fundamentally, it involves accepting and loving yourself as you are.

Ways Of working on Self-Esteem

As stated previously, enhancing your self-esteem requires effort and time, but it is well worth the effort, as there is an undeniable correlation between high self-esteem and personal happiness. Several techniques that can assist you in contemplating yourself include the following:

Acknowledge Commendations

On second thought, hear the wish to redirect acclaim and allow it in. Strangely, research indicates a direct correlation between difficulty tolerating compliments and low self-esteem.

### Provide Yourself With a Break

Forgive your mistakes and eliminate your negative self-speculations and self-talk. Nobody is perfect or cherishes every aspect of themselves. Attempt not to expect that of yourself. When you begin a negative spiral, ask yourself if you are generally reasonable for yourself or if you are being practical.

### Love Yourself Despite Your Flaws

Indeed, there may be aspects of yourself that you wish were different, that you need to alter, or with which you are simply dissatisfied; despite this, love and respect yourself regardless.

### Respect the Individual You Are

Expect to recognize and appreciate who you are now because you are on the correct track. Determine and take pride in what makes you unique, cheerful, and esteemed.

### Understand the Significance of High Self-Esteem

When you begin to understand how your perspective on yourself affects your life satisfaction and prosperity, you may be persuaded to alter your reasoning and value yourself more.

### Search for Support

Treatment, such as mental conduct treatment, can assist you in resolving issues that may be impeding your positive self-perspective and in developing the skills necessary to interrupt negative self-talk and achieve a more optimistic outlook on yourself.

Commence Keeping a Gratitude Journal

Record in a gratitude journal all the positive aspects of your daily life, the things you like about yourself, and the accomplishments or qualities you're proud of, and then read it when you're having a negative outlook on yourself.

Be Aware of Your Thoughts

At the point when negative ones emerge, effectively determine whether to address them or to let them pass.

When you have positive considerations, you should aim to amplify them, particularly when less-than-ideal considerations arise.

### Consider Yourself to Be a Friend

As you evaluate a companion, you will likely be more forgiving, kind, empowering, powerful, and delighted than you are of yourself. Thus, whenever you are berating yourself, take a step back, alter your perspective, and view yourself as you would a friend.

### Strive to Improve Yourself

Consider what changes you can make if there are aspects of yourself or your life that you do not feel significantly improved about. Then, at that time, make arrangements to put these modifications into action. Self-esteem is essential for happiness in life. For some, this perspective may come naturally, whereas for others, it may be more of a struggle. Fortunately, regardless of where you are on the self-esteem spectrum, you can work on your vision, support, compassion, and affection for yourself. In the end, the relationship you have with yourself may be the one that makes the most impact; it provides you with the flexibility, certainty, thoughtfulness, inspiration, and love that illuminates the rest of your life and helps you become the best person you can be.


- Begin uttering "no"

Individuals with low self-esteem frequently feel compelled to say "yes" to others, even if they would prefer not to. The risk is becoming overburdened, angry, incensed, and disheartened. In general, stating no does not irritate relationships. It may be useful to continue saying no, albeit in different methods, until they get the message.

### Administer yourself a challenge

On occasion, we as a group feel apprehensive or reluctant to complete tasks. However, individuals with high self-esteem do not let these feelings prevent them from trying new things or tackling challenges. Introduce a goal, such as enrolling in an activity class or attending a social engagement. Accomplishing your goals will aid in boosting your self-esteem.

## Chapter 8: What Your Adolescent Daughter Is Hiding From You

Numerous parents discuss at length how their adolescent daughters have become estranged over the years and have stopped sharing everything with them. The parents frequently compare their adolescent daughters to their younger selves, who were vivacious and eager to share the world's wonders with their parents. It is pertinent to convey the concept of "the burden of knowledge" here. This concept is frequently used in academic circles, but it applies precisely here as well.

Usually, when we comprehend a difficult concept such as a scientific theory, we forget how things were before we comprehended it. We forget how difficult it was to comprehend the new information and how we struggled with unfamiliar, complex concepts. This causes us to believe that the concept is simple, and as a result, we are unable to empathize with those who do not comprehend the concept.

Now, let's apply the burden of knowledge concept to this situation. Most of us ignore the problems that plagued us as adolescents once we reach adulthood. We prefer to believe that adolescence was a glorious time when we had no responsibilities and enjoyed ourselves with our friends. However, the actuality was quite different. As adolescents, many of us may have struggled with self-acceptance and been victims of bullying. As a consequence, we may have displayed rebellious tendencies and distanced ourselves from our adult caregivers. As a first step, let's attempt to recall our experiences as adolescents and put ourselves in their shoes for a moment. Remember that they may be coping with more severe problems, as social media and the internet present additional obstacles.

A teenager's cultural anticipations

We grow up in a society that portrays adolescence as a challenging time for both the adolescent and the parent. In popular culture, phrases such as "teenage tantrums" and "troublesome teenager" are commonplace. Even though there is scientific support for these claims, the fact remains that we can make the teenage years simpler for our children. This cultural burden falls more heavily on teenage females than on teenage boys. The anxiety surrounding their sexual maturation may be the most significant factor, but it will only make your teen's life more wretched. It is essential to recognize that psychologists and behavioral experts have identified distinct phases of adolescent development. These must be carefully evaluated to determine how to assist them in overcoming the phase and maturing into a successful and content adult.

Even though teenagers do not conduct identically across the globe, there may be similarities in their behavioral patterns due to biological, social, and cultural factors. In spite of the common belief that adolescence begins at the age of 13, the onset of adolescence may occur earlier in modern times, when children are exposed to cultural and social factors that exacerbate rebellious tendencies. Consideration should also be given to the fact that children tend to reach puberty as early as 10 or 11, and as a result may exhibit adolescent characteristics earlier. However, there are certain symptoms that can help you recognize when your daughter is entering this phase.

The very first symptom is a desire to be regarded as an adult and an aversion to everything that is commonly associated with minors. This can include refusing certain foods, practices, or garments that they may have previously used. This could progress from moderate disinterest to a vociferous and defiant refusal to do anything an adult suggests. This is the most common phase among adolescents, as well as the most common phase in which parents or caregivers respond with aggression or control.

While we subconsciously use phrases such as "acting like a teenager," they will believe that their phase of development is abnormal and strange. We must convince them that adolescence is a normal phase of development, and we must validate their feelings and emotions. In spite of the fact that this does not equate to endorsing everything they do, it is essential to allow them a certain amount of latitude to make informed decisions in their lives. This will aid in the development of their self-efficacy, which is crucial for becoming a self-confident and self-empowered individual.

Self-efficacy is a psychological concept developed by Albert Bandura that can be defined as confidence in one's own abilities. A person with high self-efficacy is more likely to endure hardships and adversity in their lives, as they are more confident in their ability to overcome obstacles. By instilling in your child a strong sense of self-efficacy, you are inadvertently facilitating their success in life. However, a balance must be achieved prior to agreeing to all of their decisions. Teenagers are likely to make poor choices, and while they should be able to learn from them, it is our responsibility to ensure that these errors do not have severe consequences. Let's examine an illustration to better comprehend how we can assist our children in making better, more informed decisions.

If your adolescent desires to make personal decisions regarding their academics and career, it is best to guide them in this direction after a thorough discussion. By conversing with them about the subject, you will be able to determine whether their decisions are motivated by a genuine interest or passion for the subject. Inform them of alternative options and share your adolescent experiences in a friendly manner. However, it is preferable to defer to their judgment after informing them of alternative options.

Do not use phrases such as "In this house, only my opinion matters" or "As long as you depend on me, you must obey my orders" if your teenager wants to make a decision about the type of clothing she wants to wear. These types of extreme responses will only encourage further defiance. As they are already burdened with high levels of insecurity, it is crucial not to make them feel invalidated or doubt their agency.

However, modern parents and caregivers are beset by a second issue that negatively impacts the mental health and well-being of their adolescent daughters. Their dependence on social media platforms is the cause. It is normal to be concerned about the daily reports of adolescent suicides and crimes associated with social media use. However, the first step in easing your concerns is to discover what your adolescent daughter is not telling you about her social media use.

# Chapter 9: Developing The Right Attitude

The importance of having the correct mindset is so great that you must be able to live your life on purpose. But how can one acquire the proper mindset? The solution is straightforward: be optimistic!

Would you say the majority of your thoughts are negative or positive if you were asked to listen to them all?

Things You Should Know

Surprisingly, you are the most destructive cause of all the negative events in your existence. The majority of people are bombarded with negative ideas, and the reality is that thinking negatively is much easier than believing in a positive term. This is due to the fact that every day, we are exposed to numerous negative signals, both externally and internally, such as the news.

The real difficulty arises when you embrace this negativity as fact. You concentrate on your problems and spend many hours per day predicting bad news for yourself, which causes anxiety, confusion, and foreboding.

However, in reality, positive thinking does not require additional effort. By focusing on the positive aspects of your life, you may be able to filter out all false signals. The first step in replacing negative thoughts with positive ones is to make a decision that is simple once you are constantly reminded of the benefits it will bring to your life.

When you have a positive outlook, not only yourself but also the entire world can become vastly improved. With excellent ideas, they can serve as a sturdy barrier that protects your dreams and you from any negative circumstances. Additionally, positive thinking improves your physical and emotional well-being.

You must be self-assured and confident in order to have a positive mindset and attitude. Concentrate on your positive qualities. Discover your unique strengths and the things you have accomplished. Be confident in your awareness that change will assist you in developing and enhancing your self-esteem, and lastly, believe that you can genuinely bring about the desired change!

When you don't give negative notions a chance to influence your behavior and outlook on life, overcoming obstacles may become less difficult. Ensure that you have positive expectations daily and throughout your existence.

Identify healthier alternatives by considering the big picture. Lastly, be enthusiastic about the life goals you have set for yourself. Use them as motivation to persevere through the obstacles. The desire to achieve an objective, no matter how modest or significant, can boost one's self-esteem and confidence.

Having the correct attitude may not be easy, but if you surround yourself with positive thoughts, even the most negative events in your life cannot bring you down.

Take the time to reflect and continually seek out new opportunities. Learn the necessary lessons and move forward with greater confidence.

# CERTAINTY

Being certain is having faith in oneself and one's abilities. This is contingent on the circumstances. Confidence is attached to knowing what we should and should not do and having faith in our abilities. Children who lack apprehension may be better equipped to face challenges and feel ownership over their activities. They can experience disappointment and pledge to exert more effort in future endeavors. The more effective pupils are, the more certain they become.

Improving as a self-confident individual requires a healthy dose of self-assurance.

# THINGS TO KNOW AND DO THAT WILL INCREASE YOUR CONFIDENCE

1. On some matters, everyone has a shaky outlook.

Indeed, this is true for everyone, even those who have their lives completely under control; they all have areas they find challenging. Do not assume momentarily that they do not, as it is essential to human existence.

2. YOUR OWN THOUGHT PROCESS IS MORE IMPORTANT THAN ANY OTHER AVAILABLE EVALUATION OF YOU.

Maintaining a daily existence where others' evaluation of you comes first is a precarious and catastrophic position to be in. Certain individuals are grounded; they have a genuine and cherished opinion of themselves based on what they know to be true and not on the thoughts of others. Try not to allow others to influence your sense of self-worth.

3. YOU Are Sufficient in Every Case.

Regardless of how others treat you, the number of friends you have, how you look, how much money you have, whether you have a disability, your sexual orientation, and regardless of how many supporters you have.

Whether you are single, not invited to a party, battling in sports, having a deformity, being underweight or overweight, as well as anything else you have experienced or are currently going through.

You are adequate.

4. It is acceptable to appear as someone else.

Try not to invest so much effort in trying to blend in and be like everyone else. Accepting your identity as it is, not as you would like it to be, is a crucial aspect of developing confidence.

5. Never will a sculpted physique satisfy YOU.

I am aware of the awe-inspiringness. This is each of the main tricks supported by the media, design, beauty, and diet industries. I pursued this one for a long time thinking, "When I have the perfect body, then I will have the perfect life." The outcome of which depends on our collective attempts at perfection.

6. YOU Should Experience Torture.

It is impossible to evade this one. Experiencing agony is an essential component of the cycle. Each time we emerge on the other side of anguish, dread, and humiliation, we gain a greater understanding of what it means to feel strong. If you allow it, each challenge will aid in the development of your self-assurance.

7. NOT ALL People WILL LIKE YOU.

Similarly to how you could survive without everyone, not everyone will like you. What a helpful discovery that was! It implies that when someone says they could do without you, it is not a joke or an inquiry into your character; do not take it literally and continue. Focus on the people who actually like and venerate you, for they are the ones who matter.

8. IT Requires Investment.

We as a whole rant about the need for more certainty, but in reality, certainty does not occur by chance. As with anything of value, it requires investment and effort, and there are no alternatives. Therefore, stop emphasizing on instilling certainty in your children; this is a marathon, not a sprint.

9. BE Conscious.

What is the relationship between graciousness and certainty? The manner in which we treat others reveals how we genuinely feel about ourselves. If you want to feel more confident and like yourself more, treat others with more kindness.

Chapter 12 of the SE. What Is Self-Esteem

Are you familiar with the confidence game? It has been shortened to "con game" because it is an obsolete term. Confidence games consist of gaining a person's trust so that you can then confuse them. This confidence is distinct from individual confidence. In some regards.

A genuine con artist relies on gaining another person's trust. They will obtain bank accounts, money, social security numbers, credit cards, and other valuable information as a result.

A true con artist is someone who works face-to-face with others and is adept at exploiting their vulnerabilities.

The true con artist is aware that a substantial number of people will believe something simply because you told them it was true.

This same philosophy applies to self-assurance. You may want to be able to persuade others that you are an amazing and confident person, even though you dislike having the confidence of an unscrupulous artist. Even more important is your ability to convince yourself of it.

According to Freud, we are what we imagine others believe of us. Consider this assertion for a moment. Then, determine what type of person others believe you to be.

What matters is not what others genuinely think of you, but what you imagine they think of you. Because self-assurance, like the confidence game, is an illusion. This is a rip-off. It is the world's largest con game, and you are the target.

If you want to be outstanding in your career or have a wonderful relationship with a new individual, you must have self-confidence. No one will be able to halt you if you do so.

Have you ever witnessed a person enter a room with extreme confidence? They are luminous. Have you ever witnessed an individual lacking in conviction enter a room? You have likely disregarded them.

You can learn to become a safer person by employing these basic techniques to exude confidence. It's quite simple: you must respect yourself and believe you can accomplish anything.

Follow these straightforward rules to begin gaining confidence immediately:

Imagine where you want to be in five years, and then visualize yourself there. Tell others your objective. Don't be ashamed to manifest your objective if it's a good one. Strive for it.

For instance, I know somebody who desired to become a writer. She was struggling to make a living, and when people asked her what she did for a living, she would always respond, "I write, but I want a real job." She never considered her job as a writer to be "real," and she played down any success.

So, this woman decided to say that she is a writer. She decided to reveal the truth, that she is a freelance writer, rather than a person who writes to pay the bills while searching for a higher position. And guess what? Offers began to pour in. Her confidence was contagious.

People will believe what you say, but you must convince yourself first.

Stop looking for someone to blame. Confidence is taking total control of your life.

Once upon a time, there was a man who was so preoccupied with blaming others for his failings that he was oblivious to the fact that his own negative energy and lack of self-confidence kept him depressed.

He blamed his supervisor for not recognizing his accomplishments. He blamed his co-workers for his own mistakes. He blamed the women he had dated for being dishonest and cheating on him.

Then, one day, he attended a confidence-building seminar.

Because he began to see himself in a different perspective, he began to modify his behavior. He stopped blaming others and began to accept personal responsibility for his actions. The situation changed for him, both at work and in his personal relationships.

Understand your Antonyeting potential. If you are good at drawing, for instance, use it every day of your life. Look for something that stands out and practice as much as possible.

Imagine you are an Antonyeting executive who must advertise a bottle of ketchup. This ketchup is identical to all others; it is made from tomatoes and has a flavor that many people like.

If you create a flyer stating, "This is a standard ketchup, but you can buy it if you want," that would be sufficient advertising. Do you believe many individuals will purchase it? Do you believe you would receive superior results if you stated, "This is the best ketchup you've ever tasted; it's soft, has a subtle flavor, and is made with the finest tomatoes"?

Nonetheless, it is the same ketchup. It sounds more enticing than the alternative. Therefore, if you wish to advertise with a standard ketchup jar, you will likely find it at the rear of the warehouse shelves.

Other condiments will stand out. However, your ketchup may be superior to those on the label. However, nobody will be aware because you will be secluded in the rear.

Do you believe that what you say about yourself is irrelevant? Are you the type of individual who believes his or her talent and body of work will advocate for themselves in the marketplace? You will experience an unpleasant awakening. You only stated this because you lack the conviction to compete with the other candidates. You have a fear of rejection.

Someone sent a manuscript to one of New York's largest publishers for amusement some time ago. A standard rejection note arrived a month later. If it had not been for the experiment, nobody would have noticed. Ernest Hemingway's "The Old Man and the Sea" was the sent manuscript.

I believe the majority of people would concur that Ernest Hemingway was a talented writer who knew how to string words together. In today's competitive and pointed world, however, a common manuscript, a common ketchup bottle, a common employee's potential, or an ordinary person will not stand out.

To be able to convey one's ideas in today's society, one must possess self-confidence. And once you have it, others will observe it and be automatically drawn to you.

Follow the advice in this book, particularly in the final chapter, and start becoming a secure individual immediately.

The entire universe is in your hands. You simply need the courage to reach out and touch it.

## 7 Stop Making Comparisons

Regarding your self-esteem, other individuals cannot serve as a benchmark. This is due to the fact that there will always be someone who appears superior or more competent than you in any aspect of life. Researchers have discovered that individuals who frequently use social media are more likely to suffer from low self-esteem. Remind yourself that people tend to share the highlights of their lives online. Your own life should be the standard, not the lives of others, because what is best for you may not be best for someone else, and vice versa. Remind yourself that you are making progress whenever you make an enhancement or prevent yourself from repeating an error.

You do you

Comparing oneself to others is a surefire way to begin feeling inferior. Focus on your own objectives and accomplishments rather than comparing them to those of others. This pressure is unnecessary for everyone!

Keep in mind that you are a restricted version of yourself, so be YOU.

8 Practice self-care

Your capacity to appreciate other facets of yourself increases as you demonstrate that you value your health. Foods that induce irritability or fatigue should be avoided. Focus your attention on your body. A healthy diet and regular exercise can also promote optimistic thinking and increase your sense of future optimism. Spending time with those who care about you can make it easier to take care of yourself. Exercise appears on virtually all of my to-do lists. However, I would be doing you a disservice if I left it off my list. In the past few years, exercising has been one of the most empowering activities for me, as it has significantly boosted my self-esteem. To obtain the benefits, you need only take a few walks per week. begins the behavior Get started. Exercise is an excellent method to increase motivation, gain experience with goal-setting, and boost confidence. As the body begins to perspire, endorphins, the feel-good hormones, are released.

Try to get adequate rest. Too little or too much sleep can significantly affect one's mood. Refer to our pages on overcoming sleep issues for more information.

Consider your diet. Eating regularly and maintaining stable blood sugar levels can affect your mood and energy levels. Visit our culinary and mood pages for more information.

Attempt to engage in physical activity. Exercising can be very beneficial for your mental health, and for some, it can also boost their self-esteem. Visit our physical activity pages for more information.

Spend time in nature. Spending time in verdant space is beneficial to one's health. Visit our nature and mental health pages for more information.

Alcohol and recreational substances should be avoided. While you may be tempted to use alcohol or recreational drugs to contend with difficult feelings about yourself, in the long run they can make you feel worse and prevent you from addressing underlying issues. For more information, see our pages on recreational substances and alcohol.


Keep in mind that adopting a healthy lifestyle and developing a positive mindset will not occur overnight. Being kind to yourself and enhancing your sense of value takes time, practice, and fortitude. But the more you advance your ideas and perspectives, the more you may be proud of who you are and what you can accomplish. You will be delighted with your progress and eager for the future.

Understanding Your Self-Esteem

Your level of self-esteem is determined by self-assurance, skill proficiency, security, a sense of belonging, and identity. Low self-esteem, high/healthy self-esteem, and inflated self-esteem are the three levels of self-esteem.

Low self-esteem

A person with low self-esteem does not feel good about themselves regardless of what others say. Low self-esteem is characterized by persistent sentiments of worthlessness, self-doubt, and self-pity. Such individuals typically have a pessimistic outlook on life.

Typically, a person with low self-esteem is extremely critical of themselves, minimizes or dismisses their positive characteristics, evaluates themselves as inadequate in comparison to their peers, and uses negative adjectives to describe themselves, such as stupid, fat, unpleasant, or unlovable.

They tend to have dialogues with themselves that are always pessimistic and self-critical, and they believe that luck plays a significant role in all of their accomplishments without taking credit for them.

When things go awry, the individual places the blame on themselves rather than considering external factors, such as the actions of other people or economic forces, over which they have no control. Do not trust someone who praises them. Low self-esteem can diminish a person's quality of life in numerous ways, including:

Persistent cynical views

Self-criticism can result in perpetual feelings of anxiety, pessimism, dread, anger, shame, or remorse.

Relationship crises, including

Because they believe they are unlovable, they may put up with all manner of outrageous behavior from partners.

Alternately, low self-esteem leads to hostility and a propensity to harass others.

This individual may have doubts about their abilities and avoid challenges out of fear.

A person with perfectionism may overachieve in order to mitigate for what they perceive as their inferiority.

Fear of being appraised – they may avoid activities involving other people out of concern they will be negatively evaluated. The individual feels self-conscious and isolated in social situations and frequently searches for 'signs' that others dislike them.

Low stability – a person with low self-esteem finds it difficult to endure a challenging life event because they view themselves as "hopeless" already.

Absence of self-care – the individual may care so little for themselves that they fail to take appropriate care of themselves or engage in self-abuse, such as excessive alcohol consumption and smoking.

# Chapter 9: Do Not Contrast Yourself With Others And The World Around You.

People feel apprehensive and discontent because they frequently compare themselves to others. If you are among them, you must abandon this unhealthy practice. Theodore Roosevelt once said that comparison robs happiness.

Stop Comparing Yourself to Others

You must reevaluate yourself in order to cease this unhealthy habit. Who do you most frequently compare yourself to? These individuals may be your coworkers, classmates, siblings, or acquaintances.

Consider the individuals to whom you have made comparisons within the past twenty-four hours. Recall your most recent Instagram or Facebook login. Which new information left you feeling apprehensive or envious? In contrast, which updates made you feel superior or superior to others?

People have compared themselves to others since the beginning of time. This is not unusual. Nonetheless, it is equally toxic.

To break this unhealthy tendency, you must refrain from mindlessly scrolling through social media. Investigate the effects of social media on individuals. You can search for studies, for instance, that demonstrate how social media updates foster sentiments of envy. By understanding these negative effects, you can be encouraged to cease using social media and begin living your life.

The following are some suggestions you may find useful:

1. Recognize your triggers and avoid them whenever possible.

Observe the circumstances that cause you to begin comparing yourself to others. Social media platforms are detrimental to the health of many individuals. Observe how social media affects your emotions.

Do you immediately feel terrible when you visit Facebook, Twitter, or Instagram and see someone posting about their day? Do you feel envious whenever you see their vacation, family, or technology-related social media posts? Do you feel inferior when you read about a friend's promotion on social media?

If using social media makes you feel bad, you should cease using it. If you are unable to refrain from logging in, you may deactivate your account. If you believe deleting it would be excessive, you can deactivate it. The point is that you must minimize your exposure to social media updates.

Certain activities outside the home may make you feel ill. For example, do you feel resentful when you visit the mall and see people shopping for new items? Do expensive vehicles in the parking lot make you feel bad about your financial situation?

If you feel normal before seeing any of these items, then going to these locations is a trigger. Therefore, you must avoid frequenting this location. If you need to make a purchase, you should refrain from observing the individuals around you. You can also take a different route to avoid traveling by the shopping center.

In addition, you should make a list of the people, locations, and things that may provoke envy or comparison. Write down the negative effects they have on you. Determine potential alternatives to your comparison triggers.

Remember that external appearance and internal characteristics are not comparable.

It is not a good practice to judge individuals solely on the basis of their physical appearance. This applies, among other things, to intelligence, riches, relationships, and family life.

A person who flaunts costly items in public, for instance, may be broke. A couple who frequently posts photos of themselves may have relationship issues.

In general, individuals craft the public versions of their existence. You must continue to wish others well. However, you should not punish yourself because you believe you are not performing well enough. Consider that you do not know what goes on behind closed doors.

Remember that contentment cannot be purchased with money.

Yes, money can purchase items that may contribute to pleasure. For instance, it can be used to purchase a residence for your family or pay for your education. However, money cannot buy pleasure on its own. This is why you should not allow it to dominate your existence.

Be diligent with your task, but do not let it consume your life. Spend time with colleagues and family. Participate in activities such as hobbies and athletics. Do not devote all of your waking hours to developing your business or working. There is a great deal more to life than making money.

4. Be appreciative of your blessings and practice being content.

When individuals receive blessings, they frequently desire more. Instead of being grateful and content with what they have, they believe it is insufficient. Additionally, they begin to compare themselves to others.

Therefore, you must continually remind yourself of the positive aspects of your existence. Be grateful for even the smallest of your benefits. Be appreciative of the food you consume, the water you drink, and the shelter that protects you from the elements. Be appreciative of your family, friends, employment, and opportunities.

Consider what would happen if you lost everything you currently possess. For example, would you feel uneasy if your electricity or water supply was disconnected? Would you be devastated if a deluge damaged your home? What if you lose your employment or a member of your family?

If you consider the consequences of losing your current possessions, you will appreciate them more. People have a tendency to neglect their blessings because they take them for granted.


Turn your propensity of comparison into motivation.

Even negative things can be transformed into something positive. Therefore, you should not feel envious if you observe others obtaining good fortune. Instead, determine that you also wish to receive positive outcomes.

For instance, if you heard that a coworker was promoted, you could work harder to achieve the same result.

Do not squander time feeling resentful or angry. If you see an old acquaintance posting on Facebook about his booming business, you should not feel resentful. You should instead feel encouraged and motivated to start your own business.

## Chapter 10: Comprehensive Therapeutic Assistance For Low Self-Esteem

Did you know that 89% of those who have been harassed believe it has negatively impacted their confidence?

Still uncertain as to whether you have low self-esteem?

It is perfectly normal to have a pessimistic outlook on yourself from time to time, but if this sensation is persistent, you may have low self-esteem.

Low self-esteem can negatively impact your emotional health, your decisions regarding your appearance, and your future.

It's difficult to like every aspect of your appearance, but dwelling on flaws can seriously undermine your confidence.

Additional consequences of diminished self-esteem include:

You avoid problematic situations.

Anxiety.

Sensitive to feedback.

You have difficulty trusting yourself.

Removing oneself from social situations.

It is essential to recognize where transformation is possible.

Change is not assured to occur effectively or promptly, but it is possible.

## HERE ARE THE MOST EFFECTIVE WAYS TO BUILD YOUR SELF-ESTEEM

### CONFRONT NEGATIVE THOUGHTS ABOUT YOURSELF.

Replace them with additional positive thoughts that laud your strengths; you can do this by listing at least three things with which you get along well.

This list will assist you in returning to reality when you begin to feel depressed.

Take good care of yourself.

Eating well and exercising stimulates endorphins, the body's natural sedatives, which inspire confidence and a more positive outlook.

When you exercise, you will relieve stress and sleep better. Thinking about yourself, having a chaotic dance in your room, or running around the block are extraordinary methods for boosting your confidence.

3. RELAX

Consistent tension can play a significant role in low confidence, as it increases the frequency of negative thoughts, lowers your confidence, and leaves you too exhausted to act.

Consider working out, being social, and engaging in many of your favorite activities.

This can be anything from housekeeping, meditation, gaming, indoor moving, singing, etc.; if it helps you, it helps!

## 4. SET GOALS

Take the time to reflect on your goals on a consistent basis. Then, establish daily objectives that are reasonable and track your progress by keeping track of your accomplishments.

This can be as simple as polishing a piece of work or tidying up (and this can be a skill test for all of us!). When you have completed every item on your afternoon to-do list, you will experience a tremendous sense of accomplishment.

Try not to be impeded by the schedule; occasionally you will not be able to complete everything, and that's okay! Everyone has off days; perhaps create a shorter schedule for the following day and assess your performance.

## 5. HELP SOMEONE OUT

This can be a friend, relative, or even a classmate who is struggling with their work or creating some intense school memories.

It's amazing how much our confidence is bolstered when we do selfless acts - do one thing per week to assist another without expecting anything in return.

6. Adopt a different viewpoint

Examine precarious situations from alternative vantage points. Replace "why should I bother?" with "I won't know unless I try."

By looking at a situation from a more realistic perspective, you'll realize that you can do what you want; you just need a little more motivation. By doing this each time you have a negative thought, you'll eventually default to this type of energy on the regular, and who doesn't love a hard worker? Occasionally, we simply need to consider and try different things to overcome low confidence.

7. TRY NEW THINGS

Our minds are excellent at acquiring new information, and the more new information we acquire, the better we become at acquiring it, and the more likely it is that we will discover things that we are passionate about.

Everyone requires a creative outlet; music, craftsmanship, dance, games, sewing, cooking, website architecture - you can easily find instructional videos on YouTube. There exists all the data you desire; all that remains is for you to view it.

## 8. SURROUND YOURSELF WITH POSITIVE-FEELING PEOPLE

Sometimes our companions don't encourage us, and that's perfectly acceptable; you simply need to invest your energy with those who value and consider you more frequently.

These do not need to be your friends, but could be relatives, online friends, or neighbors, as well as those friends who are not assisting your mindset. Determine if they are a pernicious companion and consider limiting your association with those who cause you to deeply regret your actions.

Even if they're the most popular kid in school or the best person you know, it's not worth your time if they make you feel like garbage!

### 9. ACCEPT YOURSELF

No one is superior. We as a whole have problems and we all have flaws. Figure out how to acknowledge and appreciate your 'flaws' or flaws, as they make you unique. So, get to work, honey!

Self-recognition is the path to certainty. When people offer you compliments, you should simply express gratitude instead of ignoring them or responding negatively.

Keep visual reminders of positive experiences.

Keepsakes are an excellent way to remember all the interesting things you have been doing.

What about creating a'mass of distinction' with photographs of you and your friends? Always carrying a camera in our pockets, we should take more photographs. When you reflect on these moments, you will realize how many amazing things you've accomplished this year.

# Chapter 11: Avoiding The Negative Behaviors That Will Ruin Your Child's Life

Raise your standards of expectation. Think highly of your child and compliment his accomplishments with phrases such as "great report card," "great game," and "you have an excellent character judge when choosing friends." This demonstrates to your twin or adolescent that you recognize the positive contributions he makes to his life, not just the negative ones. He is aware that you are pleased of him, and he will strive to continue making you proud because he desires your approval. You can steer him in the wrong direction of decisions just as readily by making negative comments to or about him. For instance, if your adolescent overhears you labeling him negatively, such as stupid, evil, cruel, dishonest, etc. This is precisely how they will determine to begin acting, and bad behavior will then ensue. The same applies to generalized statements about adolescents, such as "all adolescents experiment with beer." Then why not drink beer, and if he gets caught, you will regret those remarks because you gave them permission to consume alcohol.

Pick your battles wisely. As a parent of an adolescent, you will engage in numerous significant disagreements. If you choose to dispute about every single detail, you are being a pest to them. If you consider the big picture, you may decide to let them win the small things so you can participate in the big stuff. Otherwise, all they will hear when you speak is "blah blah blah" as they respectfully muffle you out.

It is a scientific fact that hormones are a problem between the ages of 10 and 20; therefore, hormones should not be used as a panacea. What is not a scientific fact is that these hormones have little impact on the majority of children, or at least not enough to be used as an excuse for poor behavior. Therefore, do not use "it's just hormones" as an excuse for your teen's behavior; do not simply attribute it to hormones. Instead of blaming hormones if your adolescent seems agitated or upset for no apparent reason, ask them what's wrong. They may not have the response you want to hear, particularly if they remain silent, but they will know that you love them enough to have noticed and are available if they want to talk. That can make the world of difference for an adolescent. Oftentimes, it is stress at school, an issue with a friend, or a problem with a person of the opposite sex, and the vast majority of the time, they will return and speak to you, or they will resolve the issue in a healthy manner.

Ø You must find a healthy balance; most of the time, parents of misbehaving preteens and teenagers fall into one of two extreme categories. They act out with bad behavior to prove to their parents that they are not required to heed to them because they are overly controlling and suffocating. They are striving for independence so that they can begin the maturation process. The opposite are parents who allow their children to do whatever they please. These adolescents will exhibit poor discernment in their behavior choices because they believe no one cares, so why not?

Children and adolescents of all ages not only require rules and boundaries, but also desire them. They need structure in their lives and someone who cares enough about them to enforce those rules, because without that their lives are chaotic and they are not emotionally prepared to handle any of this. According to research, children whose parents have not established any boundaries or rules are three times more likely to begin drinking at a young age. They are also more sexually active and more likely to become dependent on prescription drugs that likely escaped their parents' medical cabinet. The sad truth is that children of overly strict parents were twice as likely to use illegal substances, contract sexually transmitted diseases, and drink. The answer is straightforward: be fair and reasonable. The punishment must be proportional to the offense; a child cannot be grounded for a month for being 10 minutes late to curfew. If they do not return home at all, you can, of course.

Ø Know who your tween/teen is associating with; familiarize yourself with their peers. You can ask as many questions as you want, but one thing is certain: you may only be receiving part of the story. Therefore, you should always meet their friends, and knowing their parents is never a poor idea. Always make your residence the epicenter for sleepovers and after-school hangouts. This provides you the opportunity to observe: a) Who they are associating with?

b) What is their relationship with their friend?

Be a sophisticated mother. Whom all of your teen's peers adore, who provides the best snacks and dinner, and with whom they all enjoy conversing. Your adolescent will enjoy this. They find it extremely cool that their peers like their mother, and they would like to hang out with their friends at home. Utilize social media to your advantage and become social media peers with your preteens and teenagers. This should be a house rule for anyone under the age of 16: "Mom must be your friend, or you cannot use social media." You are not required to interact with them or make any comments; simply linger in the background and observe what is occurring. Anything that makes you feel uneasy should be addressed in person, not on Facebook. Keep abreast of what is occurring. This is the most effective method to ensure that nothing is inappropriate. Additionally, you may be able to save some excellent photographs of your child; they take and post the finest selfies.

Ø Try to maintain a relationship with your adolescent; obviously, this is a working age for this group. Girls are preoccupied attempting to age themselves with their hair and makeup. They are attempting to appear mature by showing off in front of their peers and relying heavily on their cell phones. Boys are boys, and oh, how entertaining they can be! They spend the same amount of time in front of the mirror as teenage females because they must check for facial hair growth. In front of their peers, they spend a great deal of time flaunting their cell phone prowess and flexing their small muscles. No matter how busy you are, as parents of teenagers, it is crucial that you maintain contact with them during this stage of their existence. They require your presence far more than they will ever acknowledge, so you must simply be present. Plan a special night out with your teenage daughter, including an early dinner, a journey to the mall, and a chick flick. Ask her about her preferences. The only rule is that you and she must enjoy yourselves. The same two rules apply to your adolescent son: give him a choice of activities, and propose dinner and bowling or a movie.

Make it mandatory that families consume dinner together at least five out of seven nights per week, unless someone has to work. Family dinners are the best method to maintain relationships.

Teach them to deal with tension; we often view them as "babies," and what possible stress could they have at this age? Well, although they are not yet paying mortgages, they do have concerns that are equally essential to them at this age. They worry about passing exams, S.A.T.s, which institution they will attend, global warming, ailing parents, girl problems, boy problems, life, and death. You name it, they are concerned about it. As their parents, we must assist them in managing the stressors in their lives so that they do not resort to smoking, drinking, or substance use to cope with problems in life. Start by being a good example; don't drink in front of your children, and smoking conveys the message that it's acceptable for them to do so as well. Children learn more from your actions than from your words, so never do anything that you would not want your child to do.

Raising a child is unquestionably the hardest task you will ever have, but also the most rewarding. There are no explicit instructions or regulations. When it comes to childrearing, our only true resources are gut instinct and the advice of those who have gone before us.

This journey will result in an independent, productive member of society who is also affectionate and kind.

You will be just as proud of them throughout their lifetimes as you were when they first pooped in the toilet on their own, because they were and will always be your babies.

www.ingramcontent.com/pod-product-compliance
Lightning Source LLC
Chambersburg PA
CBHW050249120526
44590CB00016B/2275